Cuba

by Robin S. Doak

Content Adviser: Sandra Levinson,
Executive Director, Center for Cuban Studies,
New York, New York

Reading Adviser: Dr. Linda D. Labbo,
Department of Reading Education, College of Education,
The University of Georgia

COMPASS POINT BOOKS
MINNEAPOLIS, MINNESOTA

FIRST REPORTS

Compass Point Books
3109 West 50th Street, #115
Minneapolis, MN 55410

Visit Compass Point Books on the Internet at *www.compasspointbooks.com*
or e-mail your request to *custserv@compasspointbooks.com*

On the cover: Morrow Castle walls in Havana, Cuba

Photographs ©: James Davis; Eye Ubiquitous/Corbis, cover; U.S. Department of Education/Peter Manzelli,
4, 27, 42–43; Bruce Coleman Inc./Dannielle Hayes, 6, 7, 25, 41; Wolfgang Kaehler/www.wkaehlerphoto.com,
8; North Wind Picture Archives, 9, 12; Stock Montage, Inc., 10, 11; Hulton/Archives by Getty Images,
13, 14, 17, 18, 19, 34; Index Stock Imagery/Jan Halaska, 15; Jorge Rey/Getty Images, 16, 26; Durand
Patrick/Corbis Sygma, 21; Bruce Coleman Inc./Pat Canova, 22; Tom Stack & Assoc./Mark Newman, 23,
24; Index Stock Imagery/Frank Staub, 29; Franco Origlia/Getty Images, 30–31, 32; Daniel Laine/Corbis,
33; Reuters NewMedia Inc./Corbis, 35; Tim Page/Corbis, 36; Kevin Fletcher/Corbis, 37; AP Photo/David
Longstreath, 38; Bill Nation/Corbis Sygma, 39; Index Stock Imagery/Lou Jones, 40.

Editor: Patricia Stockland
Photo Researcher: Marcie C. Spence
Designer/Page Production: Bradfordesign, Inc./Biner Design
Cartographer: XNR Productions, Inc.

Library of Congress Cataloging-in-Publication Data
Doak, Robin S. (Robin Santos), 1963–
    Cuba / by Robin Doak.
        p. cm. — (First reports)
    Summary: An introduction to the geography, history, culture, and people of this island country
    in the West Indies.
    Includes bibliographical references and index.
    ISBN 0-7565-0580-1 (hardcover)
    1. Cuba—Juvenile literature. [1. Cuba.] I. Title. II. Series.
    F1758.5.D63 2004
    972.91—dc22   2003014430

Table of Contents

*NOTE: In this book, words that are defined in the glossary are in **bold** the first time they appear in the text.*

Hola!

"Hola! Bienvenidos!" People in Cuba might welcome you with these words. Hola is the Spanish word for "hello." Bienvenidos means "welcome." Spanish is the language that is spoken in Cuba.

▲ *Classmates on a field trip welcome you to Cuba.*

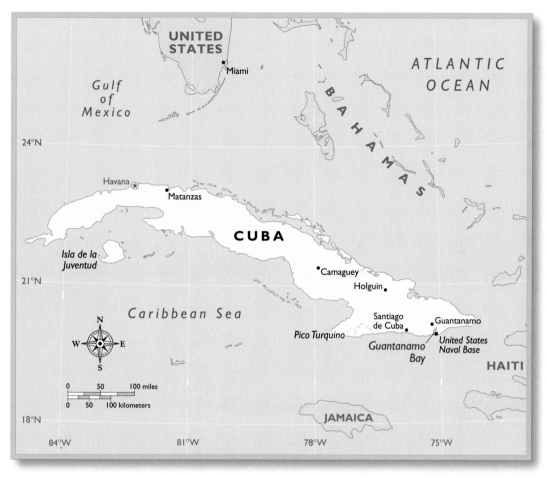

▲ *Map of Cuba*

The Republic of Cuba is an island nation in the Caribbean Sea. The country is made up of a main island and thousands of tiny islands. Cuba is the largest and westernmost island in the Caribbean. It is slightly smaller in area than the U.S. state of

Pennsylvania. Cuba's neighbors to the north are the Bahamas and the United States. Miami, Florida, is only 90 miles (144 kilometers) from Cuba. The island of Jamaica is south of Cuba. The island of Haiti is Cuba's neighbor to the east. Mexico lies to the west.

▲ *The Capitol in Havana was once the nation's capitol building. It now houses the Academy of Science.*

Land and Weather

▲ *Shoreline along southeastern Cuba*

Cuba is a beautiful, tropical country. Its coasts are lined with sandy beaches and rocky cliffs. Most of the land is flat, with gently rolling plains and low hills. In the southeast, however, rugged mountains stretch into the sky. The country's highest peak is Pico Turquino. It is more than 6,500 feet (1,983 meters) high.

Cuba's climate is tropical, but it's cooler than most countries near the **equator.** This is because Cuba receives westerly **trade winds.** The country has two seasons: the dry season, from November through April, and the wet season, from May through October. During the wet season, Cuba receives tropical storms. Every one or two years, there is a hurricane.

Cuba is home to many different animals and plants. There are few large animals on the island, but there are many types of colorful birds, including parrots and hummingbirds. The island is covered with palm trees, jasmine, and other tropical plants.

◀ *The bird of paradise flower can be found in Cuba.*

History of Cuba

▲ *Christopher Columbus is greeted by native Cubans.*

The first people to live in Cuba were native tribes. These tribes came to the island from Central or South America thousands of years ago. In 1492, the explorer Christopher Columbus landed in Cuba. Columbus claimed the island for Spain. For the next 400 years, Spain controlled Cuba.

Spanish settlers set up sugar **plantations.** They enslaved the native people to work in the fields. Only

100 years after Columbus arrived, the native tribes had died out because of the harsh treatment and diseases brought by the Spanish settlers. Soon the Spanish brought people from Africa to work the land as slaves. Today, most Cubans are **descendants** of these early Spanish, African, and native residents.

By the late 1860s, Cubans decided that they wanted to be free from Spanish rule. In 1868, Cubans began a

▲ *The Ten Years War did not free Cubans from Spain.*

war against Spain. The 10-year rebellion ended in defeat for the Cuban freedom fighters.

In 1898, the U.S. battleship *Maine* was blown up in Havana's harbor. The United States blamed Spain for the disaster and declared war. The Spanish-American War lasted only a few months. Spain lost the war and lost control of Cuba. In 1902, Cuba became somewhat independent. Its independence was limited by the Platt Amendment. This was a U.S. law that said the United States could step into Cuban affairs if it did not like what Cuba was doing.

◄ *The New York Journal reported on the sinking of the* Maine.

▲ *Crews work to clean up the USS* Maine *wreckage in 1898.*

After the Spanish-American War, the United States was allowed to lease a piece of land on the island. The land was located at Guantanamo Bay, on the eastern end of Cuba. The United States still operates a naval base there.

Modern Cuba

▲ *Batista ruled Cuba for many years.*

In 1933, an army officer named Fulgencio Batista seized power in Cuba. Batista was a **dictator.** He ruled Cuba harshly. Cubans elected their own president when Batista retired in 1944. However, in 1952, Batista again seized power. This led to the formation of the July 26th Movement. This group worked to overthrow Batista.

In 1959, the rebel July 26th group, led by Fidel Castro and Che Guevara, finally forced Batista from

▲ *Fidel Castro (center) in 1959, after forcing Batista from power*

power. Castro became the new leader. Under Castro's rule, Cuba became a socialist country. Socialism is a type of government in which the state owns all or most property. Castro's government took control of farmland, banks, and other businesses. Even businesses owned by Americans were taken over. As a result, the United States broke off relations with Castro and his new government.

Many Cubans were unhappy about the new government. They were afraid that Cuba would become

communist. The leaders in the United States were afraid of this, too. Many people who fought against the new government were jailed. Others who disagreed chose to leave Cuba for the United States

◀ *Che Guevara, one of the leaders of the July 26th group, was killed in a revolutionary movement in Bolivia in 1967.*

while they were still able to do so. More than 250,000 Cubans moved to the United States between 1959 and 1962.

Because the United States considers Cuba a communist country, it refuses to have full relations with Cuba. After more than four decades, Fidel Castro is still the president.

▲ *Fidel Castro meets with business people in 2003 to discuss tourism.*

Cuba and the United States

▲ *Cuban militia celebrate their victory after the Bay of Pigs invasion.*

Since 1960, Cuba and the United States have had a rocky relationship. Problems began when the Cuban government took control of American businesses on the island. In 1961, hundreds of

Cuban **exiles** living in the United States tried to invade Cuba, with the support of the U.S. government. This was called the Bay of Pigs invasion. It failed, and Castro remained in power.

In 1962, the Soviet Union sent nuclear missiles to Cuba. The missiles easily could have been fired at the

▲ *The Soviet ship* Kasimov *at sea off the coast of Cuba was seen as a threat to the United States.*

▲ *President John F. Kennedy addressing the nation during the Cuban missile crisis*

United States. President John F. Kennedy sent a
warning to the Soviets: Remove the missiles, or face
nuclear war. The weapons were finally taken out of
Cuba when the United States agreed to remove its

missiles from Turkey. The Soviet leaders felt these missiles were threatening their country.

After the Cuban missile crisis, the United States tightened an embargo against Cuba. An embargo is an order that bans something. The U.S. embargo stopped Americans from visiting or trading with Cuba. It banned Cuban goods from being sold in the United States. This embargo continues today, although there has been talk in Congress about easing it. The sale of food and medicine has been allowed since 2002. Most Americans cannot travel to Cuba unless it is for educational reasons.

The embargo has made life difficult for people in Cuba. After the Soviet Union fell apart in 1989, life became even harder. For many years, the Soviet Union had given Cuba money and support.

In Search of Freedom

▲ *Some Cubans try to enter the United States in homemade rafts.*

Each year, thousands of Cubans leave their country. These people are looking for a better life. Most Cubans want to come to the United States. Today, there are about 1.5 million Cubans living in the United States. Miami, Florida, has the largest Cuban population. About 700,000 Cuban people live there.

U.S. law allows 20,000 Cubans to enter the country legally each year. However, many people risk their lives to come illegally. Some travel in homemade rafts or small boats. Others arrive on planes or travel by land through Mexico. Those caught at sea are sometimes returned to Cuba. Those who reach land are allowed to stay. This is not true for people from other countries who enter illegally. One of the reasons Cubans are given special treatment is because of the large number of Cuban Americans in Florida. They play an important role in elections there, and their opinion counts.

The continued attempts by Cubans to enter the United States, and the return of these people to Cuba, have forced Americans to think about the problems between the two countries.

◀ *Little Havana in Miami has a large Cuban population.*

Cuba's Cities

▲ *Havana is a very crowded city.*

More than 11 million people live in Cuba. More than 2 million live in the biggest and most crowded city, Havana. Many people live in apartment buildings.

Havana is Cuba's capital. The island's government buildings are located there. The crowded city is also home to towering skyscrapers, factories, and other businesses. Outdoor markets are busy places to shop.

Havana is located on Cuba's northwest coast. It is an important port. Goods from around the island are sent to Havana by truck and train. From there, they are shipped to other countries. Goods from around the world are brought by ship into Havana's harbor.

Old Havana is a historic section of the city. Some of its ancient forts, castles, and palaces are nearly

▲ *Historic forts and castles, such as Casillo de la Real Fuerza, are located in Havana.*

400 years old! Unfortunately, many of these important old buildings are badly in need of repair. Because of the embargo, materials for repairs cannot be brought in from the United States, which would be the easiest and cheapest place to get them.

Cuba's second largest city is Santiago de Cuba. It is located on the southeast tip of the island. Santiago de Cuba is home to some of the island's oldest palaces. Other big cities in Cuba include Camaguey, Holguin, and Guantanamo.

◀ *Santiago de Cuba has beautiful architecture.*

Business in Cuba

▲ *Marketplace art displays attract tourists.*

Tourism is Cuba's number one industry. Although Americans cannot freely visit the tropical island, people from the rest of the world can. Each year, more than 1 million people from Canada, Europe, and other areas visit Cuba. They enjoy the island's sandy beaches, sparkling water, and exotic sites. Scuba diving is popular, too. Divers explore the island's coral reefs and underwater wildlife.

Farming is another important industry. Sugar is the leading crop. Each year, millions of pounds of Cuban sugar are shipped all over the world. Another valuable crop is tobacco. Cigars made from Cuban tobacco are

▲ *Tobacco, an important and famous Cuban crop, is prepared for the curing process.*

world famous. Other crops include citrus fruits, coffee, rice, and potatoes. Since 1993, Cuba has used **organic** farming to help feed its population. Castro put this program into place, and Cuba is the first nation in the world to make the successful switch.

Mining is important to Cuba's economy. Many metals are found on the island, including nickel, cobalt, iron, copper, and gold. Cuban factories make medicines, paper, foods, cement, and textiles.

Most workers in Cuba make very little money. All Cubans are given ration books called *libretas*. These allow Cubans to buy certain foods and necessary goods from the government at very low cost. Often, however, these foods and other items run out. Buying food "off the libreta" means spending more money for the same items. These are usually purchased in farmers' markets.

Education and Religion

▲ *Cuban children attend school for free.*

After Fidel Castro took power, he closed most private schools. Today, schools and universities in Cuba are public and free. All children must attend school through the 12th grade. Day care is also free for children under 7.

Many people in Cuba are Roman Catholics. Spanish settlers brought the religion to the island in the 1500s. After Castro's government took power, there were many disputes between the Catholic Church and the government. Many churches were closed, and many priests left the island. Others who fought directly against the government were jailed. In the early 1990s, restrictions on religion were eased. In 1997, Castro met with Pope John Paul II, the leader of the Roman Catholic Church, and invited him to Cuba. In 1998, Pope John Paul II came to Cuba and celebrated Mass in cities throughout the island.

◀ *A Catholic cathedral in Havana*

▲ *Santeria shrines are often decorated with colorful beads and flowers.*

Many more Cubans practice a religion that combines African and Catholic beliefs. This religion is called Santeria. People who follow Santeria believe in many saints, called *orishas.* Some have shrines in their homes to honor these saints, many of whom represent the same qualities as the Catholic saints. For example, the orisha Babalu-aye is like Saint Lazarus.

Protestant religions are also practiced in Cuba. These include Baptist, Methodist, and Presbyterian.

Cuban Culture

Cuban culture is a blend of Spanish and African customs. The Spanish brought their language, religion, architecture, and music to the island. African slaves brought their own religions and traditions.

Cuba is well known for its music. The mambo, cha-cha, and rumba are just a few of the music styles

▲ *A woman dances to a lively street rumba.*

created there. What is called salsa music in the United States is really just Cuban music. All true Cuban music combines African drums, Spanish guitars, and brass instruments. It is called *son*.

Jazz is very popular in Cuba. Many great jazz artists were born on the island. Each year, an international jazz festival is held in Havana. The island is also home to many theaters and museums, as well as a national ballet company.

Before Castro took power, Cuba was well known for its talented writers, artists, and musicians.

◄ *Many people consider musician and bandleader Pérez Prado to be the father of mambo.*

▲ *At an art festival, a Cuban boy takes in the details of a butter sculpture.*

After 1959, many new schools were built, including ones just for artists and musicians. The government also started the first film institute. With free education, today there are many more writers, artists, and musicians. They are not very well known in the United States, however, because of the difficult relationship between the two countries.

Cuban food also draws from Spanish and African influences. The most popular Cuban dishes are roast pork, black beans with rice (called *moros y cristianos*, or "Moors and Christians"), *picadillo* (ground hamburger with olives and spices), and fried bananas. Popular desserts are flan, *boniato*, and *natilla*.

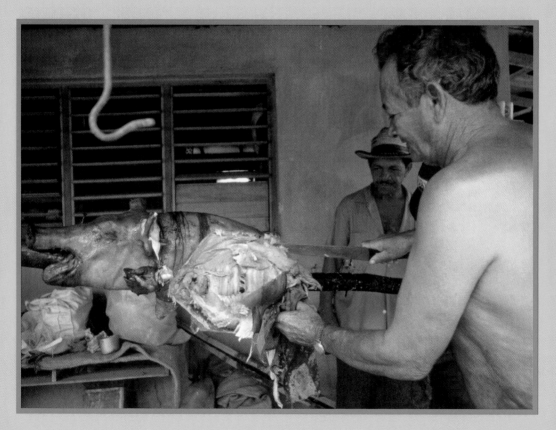

▲ *A traditional barbecue of roast pork*

Sports

▲ *In an alley in Trinidad, boys play a pick-up game of baseball.*

Cubans love sports. One of the favorite sports on the island is baseball. Each year, a championship series is held. Cuba's two top baseball teams compete to be number one. Basketball, volleyball, and soccer are also popular.

Cuban athletes have earned honors all around the world. The island is home to Olympic gold medal winners, boxing champions, and world record holders. Teofilo Stevenson won gold medals for boxing in the 1972, 1976, and 1980 Olympic Games. Ana Quirot set the world record in the 400 meters at the Pan-American Games in 1991. That was the year Cuba hosted the games.

Many Cuban athletes who now live in the United States are also famous. Livan Hernandez, who plays baseball for the Montreal Expos, helped the Florida Marlins win the World Series in 1997.

◀ *Ana Quirot at the Pan-American Games in Cuba in 1991*

Holidays and Festivals

▲ *Parades help mark important events such as Liberation Day.*

Each year on January 1, Cubans celebrate Liberation Day. This marks the day the revolutionaries came to power. On July 26, Cubans take part in the Celebration of National Rebellion. This holiday celebrates the July 26, 1953, attack on Fort Moncada in Santiago de Cuba, an early rebellion that failed. Another national holiday is the Day of Cuban Culture on October 10.

All Cubans look forward to carnival season during the summer. These big, outdoor festivals include music, dancing, colorful costumes, and parades. Cuba's most famous carnival is held in July in Santiago de Cuba. This festival got its start hundreds of years ago. It began as a way for slaves to celebrate the end of the sugar harvest.

▲ Bright costumes are often part of festivals such as this one in Plaza Vieja in Old Havana.

Cuba Today

▲ *Cubans are slowly gaining freedom to start their own businesses, such as this produce market.*

Until the early 1990s, the government controlled all businesses. In recent years, however, Cuba's government has allowed companies from around the world to come to Cuba and invest, or use their money to help grow businesses. Today, there are companies from Spain, Canada, Italy, France, Japan, and other countries. Much of the money earned by Cuban workers in these factories is turned over to the government. This money then helps the government pay for things like free education and free health care.

Cubans are now allowed to start their own businesses in some areas. Many islanders have set up home restaurants and small stores. Only family members are allowed to work in these businesses. The food and other materials must be purchased from the government. If these rules are broken, the government fines people or shuts down the business.

Cubans and Americans look forward to the day when the embargo is dropped and people can travel freely between the two countries. Cuba is a patriotic nation with a colorful history and a rich culture. Both the government and its people are moving toward sharing more of those traditions with the world.

▲ *Historic architecture and classic cars in Old Havana offer tourists a glimpse of the past.*

Glossary

communist—a system in which the government owns a country's businesses and controls the economy; a person who supports communist governments

descendants—a person's children, grandchildren, great-grandchildren, and their offspring

dictator—a ruler who takes complete control of a country, often unjustly

equator—an imaginary line around the middle of Earth

exiles—people who are forced or volunteer to leave their country for a time

organic—a natural method of farming not using any chemicals

plantations—a large farm worked by laborers who lived there

trade winds—winds that blow toward the equator almost continually

Did You Know?

- Cuba is the largest island in the West Indies.

- There are a large number of underground limestone caves in Cuba.

- Cuban cigars are not only popular around the world but also an important part of Cuban culture. The entire process of making these cigars is done by hand—from the handling of the tobacco plants in the field, through the drying and curing process, to the cutting and wrapping of the cigars.

At a Glance

Official name: Republica de Cuba (Republic of Cuba)

Capital: Havana

Official language: Spanish

National song: La Bayamesa

Area: 42,800 square miles (111,280 square km)

Highest point: Pico Turquino, 6,501 feet (1,983 m) above sea level

Lowest point: Sea level

Population: 11,224,321 (2002 estimate)

Head of government: President

Money: Peso

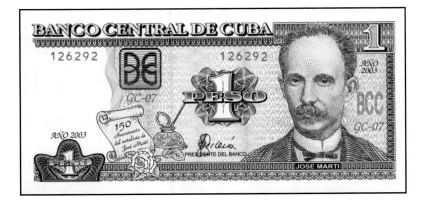

Important Dates

1492 Christopher Columbus claims the island of Cuba for Spain.

1933 Army officer Fulgencio Batista comes to power for the first time.

1959 Rebels led by Fidel Castro take control of Cuba's government.

1961 A U.S.-sponsored invasion against Castro at the Bay of Pigs fails.

1962 The Cuban missile crisis brings the United States and the Soviet Union to the brink of nuclear war.

1991 Cubans face hunger after the Soviet Union collapses, cutting off a main source of food.

1993 The government successfully puts organic farming methods into place, helping to feed the country.

1998 Pope John Paul II makes a trip to Cuba.

2002 The United States Congress passes legislation that allows food and medicine to be sent to Cuba.

Want to Know More?

At the Library

Crooker, Richard A., and Charles F. Gritzner. *Cuba*. Philadelphia: Chelsea House Publications, 2002.

McNeese, Tim. *Remember the Maine: The Spanish-American War Begins*. Greensboro, N.C.: Morgan Reynolds, 2001.

Petersen, Christine, and David Petersen. *Cuba*. New York: Children's Press, 2002.

Sonneborn, Elizabeth. *The Cuban-Americans*. San Diego: Lucent Books, 2001.

On the Web

For more information on Cuba, use FactHound to track down Web sites related to this book.

1. Go to www.compasspointbooks.com/facthound
2. Type in this book ID: 0756505801
3. Click on the *Fetch It* button.

Your trusty FactHound will fetch the best Web sites for you!

Through the Mail

Center for Cuban Studies
124 W. 23rd St.
New York, NY 10011
212/242-0559
For more information about Cuban life, culture, and history

On the Road

University of Miami Lowe Art Museum
1223 Dickinson Drive
Coral Gables, FL 33146
305/284-3438
To visit the entire collection from the Cuban Museum of the Americas

About the Author

Robin S. Doak has been writing for children for more than 14 years. A former editor of Weekly Reader and U*S*Kids magazine, Ms. Doak has authored fun and educational materials for kids of all ages. Some of her work includes biographies of explorers such as Henry Hudson and John Smith, as well as other titles in this series. Ms. Doak is a past winner of the Educational Press Association of America Distinguished Achievement Award. She lives with her husband and three children in central Connecticut.